THE WISDOM OF THE APOSTLES

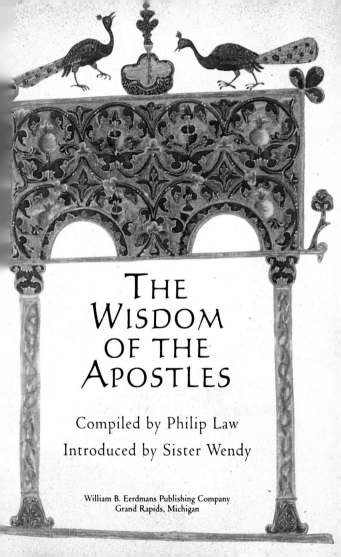

THE WISDOM OF THE APOSTLES

Compiled by Philip Law

Introduced by Sister Wendy

William B. Eerdmans Publishing Company
Grand Rapids, Michigan

This edition copyright © 1997 Lion Publishing

This edition published 1997 in the USA
through special arrangement with
Lion Publishing by
Wm. B. Eerdmans Publishing Co.
255 Jefferson Ave. S.E., Grand Rapids,
Michigan 49503

Printed in Singapore

01 00 99 98 97   7 6 5 4 3 2 1

ISBN 0-8028-3852-9

CONTENTS

INTRODUCTION

The apostles really knew Jesus. It was not because they had seen him in action and listened to him. St Paul, for instance, only saw him once, in a dramatic vision, and the gospels show us how very little the followers of Jesus actually understood him. Right to the end, at the last supper itself, we hear Jesus saying sadly to Philip, 'Have I been with you all this time and you still do not know me?' When the arrest came, shortly after, in the Garden of Gethsemane, the apostles revealed their tragic lack of true understanding and all ran away from the Lord. It was only afterwards when Jesus had ascended and sent the Holy Spirit, the spirit of truth, that his disciples at last began to know him. They pondered over what they had seen and heard and had been told by others; they prayed to understand; they held out to him their longing hearts. To this prayer, this desire to know who Jesus is, the Father is never deaf. We can know Jesus just as the apostles did, if that is what we want.

Followers of Jesus come to this blessed knowledge by expressing their need for him in prayer and by reading the Bible. Here, distilled in the words of scripture is the way, the truth and the life – words Jesus used to define what he was and what we can find in him. But the words of scripture are so rich, so dense with holy meaning, so infinite in their levels of revelation that we can easily miss their depths. A little book of extracts is ideal.

We can keep it in our pockets or handbags, have it ready on our desks or bedside tables. We can read a little, let it sink in, marvel at it, live on it. Every word is, in one sense, a judgement: do we show in our daily lives the truth we have read? But it is also a promise: the grace of God will give us these attitudes of love if we set ourselves to desire them. All richness and beauty are here, spread out for us, freely offered. What we have to do is have faith, rest trustingly on the heart of our Father, and long in will for Jesus to be able to praise the Father within us. I say 'in will' because we may not feel this desire: we may only feel the divided anxious mind that St Paul describes so feelingly in extract 19. But he ignored the weak flesh and clung in faith to the spirit of Jesus, and God's grace can empower us to do the same. The 'wisdom of the Apostles' was to know Jesus and to have his mind (see extract 25). Remember what the Lord himself said, 'Ask and you shall receive.'

SISTER WENDY

THE WISDOM
OF THE SPIRIT

A Gift from God

If any of you is lacking in wisdom,
ask God, who gives to all
generously and ungrudgingly,
and it will be given you.

But ask in faith, never doubting,
for the one who doubts is like
a wave of the sea,
driven and tossed by the wind.

James 1:5–6

WISDOM FROM ABOVE

The wisdom that is from above is first pure,
then peaceable, gentle,
and easy to be intreated,
full of mercy and good fruits,
without partiality, and without hypocrisy.

James 3:17

GOD'S FOOLISHNESS

God in his wisdom made it impossible for people to know him by means of their own wisdom. Instead, by means of the so-called 'foolish' message we preach, God decided to save those who believe.

Jews want miracles for proof, and Greeks look for wisdom. As for us, we proclaim the crucified Christ, a message offensive to the Jews and nonsense to the Gentiles; but for those whom God has called, both Jews and Gentiles, this message is Christ, the power of God and the wisdom of God.

For what seems to be God's foolishness is wiser than human wisdom, and what seems to be God's weakness is stronger than human strength.

1 Corinthians 1:21–25

SPIRITUAL DISCERNMENT

We speak of God's secret wisdom, a wisdom that has been hidden and that God destined for our glory before time began. As it is written:

'No eye has seen, no ear has heard,
no mind has conceived
what God has prepared for those
who love him' –

but God has revealed it to us by his Spirit. The Spirit searches all things, even the deep things of God. For who among men knows the thoughts of a man except the man's spirit within him? In the same way no-one knows the thoughts of God except the Spirit of God.

The man without the Spirit does not accept the things that come from the Spirit of God, for they are foolishness to him, and he cannot understand them, because they are spiritually discerned.

1 Corinthians 2:7, 9–11, 14

THE PRACTICE OF WISDOM

Whoever listens to God's word but does not put it into practice is like a man who looks in a mirror and sees himself as he is. He takes a good look at himself and then goes away and at once forgets what he looks like.

But those who look closely into the perfect law that sets people free, who keep on paying attention to it and do not simply listen and then forget it – they will be blessed by God in what they do.

James 1:23–25

THOUGHTS WORTH THINKING

Finally, brothers,
whatever is true, whatever is noble,
whatever is right, whatever is pure,
whatever is lovely, whatever is admirable —
if anything is excellent or praiseworthy —
think about such things.

Philippians 4:8

THE GRACE
OF GOD

A LIVING HOPE

Blessed be God the Father of our Lord Jesus
Christ, who in his great mercy has given us
a new birth into a living hope through the
resurrection of Jesus Christ from the dead
and into a heritage that can never be spoilt
or soiled and never fade away. It is reserved
in heaven for you who are being kept safe by
God's power through faith until the salvation
which has been prepared is revealed at the final
point of time.

1 Peter 1:3–5

8

THE SUPREMACY OF CHRIST

In Christ everything in heaven and on earth
was created, not only things visible but also
the invisible orders of thrones, sovereignties,
authorities, and powers: the whole universe
has been created through him and for him.

He exists before all things, and all things
are held together in him. He is the head of the
body, the church. He is its origin, the first to
return from the dead, to become in all things
supreme.

For in him God in all his fullness chose
to dwell.

Colossians 1:16–19

GOD'S MYSTERIOUS PURPOSE

Blessed be God the Father of our Lord Jesus Christ, who has blessed us with all the spiritual blessings of heaven in Christ. He chose us in Christ before the world was made, to be holy and faultless before him in love. Such is the richness of the grace which he has showered on us in all wisdom and insight.

He has let us know the mystery of his purpose: that he would bring everything together under Christ, as head, everything in the heavens and everything on earth. And it is in him that we have received our heritage, marked out beforehand as we were, under the plan of the One who guides all things as he decides by his own will.

Ephesians 1:3–4, 7–13

GOD'S INDESTRUCTIBLE LOVE

We do not even know how we ought to pray, but through our inarticulate groans the Spirit himself is pleading for us, and God who searches our inmost being knows what the Spirit means, because he pleads for God's people as God himself wills; and in everything, as we know, he co-operates for good with those who love God and are called according to his purpose.

For those whom God knew before ever they were, he also ordained to share the likeness of his Son, so that he might be the eldest among a large family.

With all this in mind, what are we to say? If God is on our side, who is against us? I am convinced that there is nothing in death or life, in the realm of spirits or superhuman powers, in the world as it is or the world as it shall be, in the forces of the universe… nothing in all creation that can separate us from the love of God in Christ Jesus our Lord.

Romans 8:26–31, 38–39

GOD'S TRANSCENDENT PEACE

Do not be anxious about anything,
but in everything, by prayer and petition,
with thanksgiving,
present your requests to God.

And the peace of God,
which transcends all understanding,
will guard your hearts and your minds
in Christ Jesus.

Philippians 4:6–7

PARTICIPATION IN GOD

God's divine power has given us everything we need to live a truly religious life through our knowledge of the one who called us to share in his own glory and goodness.

In this way he has given us the very great and precious gifts he promised, so that by means of these gifts you may escape from the destructive lust that is in the world, and may come to share the divine nature.

2 Peter 1:3–4

The Meaning
of Love

TRUE LOVE

If a man say, I love God,
and hateth his brother, he is a liar:
for he that loveth not his brother,
whom he hath seen, how can he love God,
whom he hath not seen?

1 John 4:20

Let brotherly love continue.
Be not forgetful to entertain strangers: for
thereby some have entertained angels unawares.

Hebrews 13:1–2

LOVE'S HARMONY

As God's chosen ones, holy and beloved, clothe yourselves with compassion, kindness, humility, meekness, and patience.

Bear with one another and, if anyone has a complaint against another, forgive each other; just as the Lord has forgiven you, so you also must forgive.

Above all, clothe yourselves with love, which binds everything together in perfect harmony.

Colossians 3:12–14

Above all, maintain constant love for one another, for love covers a multitude of sins.

1 Peter 4:8

GOD'S LOVE WITHIN US

Let us love one another, because the source of love is God.

Everyone who loves is a child of God and knows God. This is how he showed his love among us: he sent his only Son into the world that we might have life through him.

If God thus loved us, my dear friends, we also must love one another. God has never been seen by anyone, but if we love one another, he himself dwells in us; his love is brought to perfection within us.

1 John 4:7, 9, 11–12

THE LOVE OF CHRIST

If then there is any encouragement in Christ,
any consolation from love, any sharing in the
Spirit, any compassion and sympathy… let each
of you look not to your own interests, but to
the interests of others. Let the same mind be
in you that was in Christ Jesus,

who, though he was in the form of God,
did not regard equality with God as
something to be exploited,
but emptied himself,
taking the form of a slave,
being born in human likeness.
And being found in human form,
he humbled himself and became obedient
to the point of death —
even death on a cross.

Philippians 2:1, 4–8

THE GREATEST OF THE VIRTUES

If I speak in the tongues of men and of angels,
but have not love,
I am only a resounding gong
or a clanging cymbal.
If I have the gift of prophecy
and can fathom all mysteries
and all knowledge,
and if I have a faith that can move mountains,
but have not love,
I am nothing.

If I give all I possess to the poor
and surrender my body to the flames,
but have not love,
I gain nothing.
Love is patient, love is kind.
It does not envy, it does not boast,
it is not proud.
It is not rude, it is not self-seeking,
it is not easily angered,
it keeps no record of wrongs.

Love does not delight in evil
but rejoices with the truth.
It always protects, always trusts, always hopes,
always perseveres.
Love never fails.

But where there are prophecies, they will cease;
where there is knowledge, it will pass away.
For we know in part and we prophesy in part;
but when perfection comes,
the imperfect disappears.

When I was a child, I talked like a child,
I thought like a child, I reasoned like a child.
When I became a man,
I put childish ways behind me.
Now we see but a poor reflection
as in a mirror;
then we shall see face to face.
Now I know in part; then I shall know fully,
even as I am fully known.

And now these three remain:
faith, hope and love.
But the greatest of these is love.

1 Corinthians 13

PERFECT LOVE

God is love. Whoever lives in love lives in God, and God in him. In this way, love is made complete among us so that we will have confidence on the day of judgment, because in this world we are like him.

There is no fear in love. But perfect love drives out fear, because fear has to do with punishment. The one who fears is not made perfect in love.

1 John 4:16–18

THE DEFEAT
OF EVIL

WHO WILL RESCUE ME?

I know that nothing good dwells in me – my unspiritual self, I mean – for though the will to do good is there, the ability to effect it is not. The good which I want to do, I fail to do; but what I do is the wrong which is against my will; and if what I do is against my will, clearly it is no longer I who am the agent, but sin that has its dwelling in me.

I discover this principle, then: that when I want to do right, only wrong is within my reach. In my inmost self I delight in the law of God, but I perceive in my outward actions a different law, fighting against the law that my mind approves, and making me a prisoner under the law of sin which controls my conduct.

Wretched creature that I am, who is there to rescue me from this state of death?

Who but God? Thanks be to him through Jesus Christ our Lord!

Romans 7:18–25

Draw Near to God

Do you suppose that it is for nothing that the scripture says, 'God yearns jealously for the spirit that he has made to dwell in us'? But he gives all the more grace; therefore it says, 'God opposes the proud, but gives grace to the humble.'

Submit yourselves therefore to God. Resist the devil, and he will flee from you. Draw near to God, and he will draw near to you.

James 4:5–8

THE ROOT OF EVIL

Godliness with contentment is great gain.
For we brought nothing into this world,
and it is certain we can carry nothing out.
And having food and raiment let us be
therewith content.

For the love of money is the root of all
evil: which while some coveted after, they have
erred from the faith, and pierced themselves
through with many sorrows.

1 Timothy 6:6–8, 10

The Harvest of the Spirit

Be guided by the Spirit and you will not gratify the desires of your unspiritual nature. That nature sets its desires against the Spirit, while the Spirit fights against it. They are in conflict with one another so that you cannot do what you want.

But if you are led by the Spirit, you are not subject to law. The harvest of the Spirit is love, joy, peace, patience, kindness, goodness, fidelity, gentleness, and self-control. Against such things there is no law.

Those who belong to Christ Jesus have crucified the old nature with its passions and desires. If the Spirit is the source of our life, let the Spirit also direct its course.

Galatians 5:16–18, 22–25

LOVE ALL THAT IS GOOD

Hate what is evil; cling to what is good.
Be joyful in hope, patient in affliction,
faithful in prayer.
Share with God's people who are in need.
Practise hospitality.
Rejoice with those who rejoice;
mourn with those who mourn.
Live in harmony with one another.
Do not be proud,
but be willing to associate
with people of low position.
Do not repay anyone evil for evil.
If it is possible, as far as it depends on you,
live at peace with everyone.
Do not take revenge, my friends,
but leave room for God's wrath.
Do not be overcome by evil,
but overcome evil with good.

Romans 12:9, 12–13, 14–19, 21

GOD'S WILL FOR YOU

Rejoice always,
pray without ceasing,
give thanks in all circumstances;
for this is the will of God for you.
Do not quench the Spirit.
Do not despise the words of prophets,
but test everything;
hold fast to what is good;
abstain from every form of evil.
May the God of peace sanctify you entirely;
and may your spirit and soul and body
be kept sound and blameless at the coming
of our Lord Jesus Christ.
The one who calls you is faithful,
and he will do this.

1 Thessalonians 5:16–24

May mercy, peace and love be yours
in abundance.

Jude v. 2

THE
TRANSFORMATION
OF THE SOUL

DISCERNING GOD'S WILL

Do not model your behaviour on the contemporary world, but let the renewing of your minds transform you, so that you may discern for yourselves what is the will of God – what is good and acceptable and mature.

   And through the grace that I have been given, I say this to every one of you: never pride yourself on being better than you really are, but think of yourself dispassionately, recognizing that God has given to each one his measure of faith.

Romans 12:2–3

THE NEW SELF

Get rid of your old self, which made you live as you used to – the old self that was being destroyed by its deceitful desires. Your hearts and minds must be made completely new, and you must put on the new self, which is created in God's likeness and reveals itself in the true life that is upright and holy.

Do not use harmful words, but only helpful words, the kind that build up and provide what is needed, so that what you say will do good to those who hear you. And do not make God's Holy Spirit sad; for the Spirit is God's mark of ownership on you, a guarantee that the Day will come when God will set you free.

Ephesians 4:22–24, 29–30

RENEWED IN GOD'S IMAGE

You have been raised to life with Christ, so set your hearts on the things that are in heaven, not on things here on earth. For you have died, and your life is hidden with Christ in God. Your real life is Christ, and when he appears then you too will appear with him and share his glory!

This is the new being which God, its Creator, is constantly renewing in his own image, in order to bring you to a full knowledge of himself.

Colossians 3:1–4, 10

TRANSFORMED BY LIFE

Even though our physical being is gradually decaying, yet our spiritual being is renewed day after day. And this small and temporary trouble we suffer will bring us a tremendous and eternal glory, much greater than the trouble. For we fix our attention, not on things that are seen, but on things that are unseen. What can be seen lasts only for a time, but what cannot be seen lasts for ever.

For we know that when this tent we live in – our body here on earth – is torn down, God will have a house in heaven for us to live in, a home he himself has made, which will last for ever… it is not that we want to get rid of our earthly body, but that we want to have the heavenly one put on over us, so that what is mortal will be transformed by life.

2 Corinthians 4:16 – 5:1, 4

THE LIBERATION OF CREATION

The created universe is waiting with eager
expectation for God's children to be revealed.
It was made subject to frustration, not of
its own choice but by the will of him who
subjected it, yet with the hope that the
universe itself is to be freed from the shackles
of mortality and is to enter upon the glorious
liberty of the children of God.

Up to the present, as we know, the whole
created universe in all its parts groans as if in
the pangs of childbirth. What is more, we also,
to whom the Spirit is given as the firstfruits
of the harvest to come, are groaning inwardly
while we look forward eagerly to our adoption,
our liberation from mortality.

Romans 8:19–23

THE FINAL VICTORY

This is how it will be when the dead are raised to life. When the body is buried, it is mortal; when raised, it will be immortal. When buried, it is ugly and weak; when raised, it will be beautiful and strong. When buried, it is a physical body; when raised, it will be a spiritual body.

Listen to this secret truth: we shall not all die, but when the last trumpet sounds, we shall all be changed in an instant, as quickly as the blinking of an eye. For when the trumpet sounds, the dead will be raised, never to die again, and we shall all be changed... Then the scripture will come true:

'Death is destroyed; victory is complete!'
'Where, Death, is your victory?
Where, Death, is your power to hurt?'

Thanks be to God who gives us the victory through our Lord Jesus Christ!

1 Corinthians 15:42–44, 51–57

Text Acknowledgments

Extracts from the Authorised Version of the Bible (The King James Bible), the rights of which are vested in the Crown, are reproduced by the permission of the Crown's Patentee, Cambridge University Press: pages 11, 26, 36. Scriptures quoted from the Good News Bible, published by the Bible Societies/HarperCollins Publishers Ltd UK © American Bible Society, 1966, 1971, 1976, 1992: pages 12–14, 23, 43–45, 47. Scripture quotations taken from the HOLY BIBLE, NEW INTERNATIONAL VERSION. Copyright © 1973, 1978, 1984 by International Bible Society. Used by permission of Hodder & Stoughton Ltd. All rights reserved: pages 15, 22, 30, 31, 32, 38. New Jerusalem Bible © 1985 by Darton, Longman and Todd Ltd and Doubleday and Company, Inc.: pages 18, 20, 42. Scripture text marked NRSV is from the New Revised Standard Version of the Bible, copyright © 1989 by the Division of Christian Education of the National Council of the Churches of Christ in the USA: pages 10, 27, 29, 35, 39. Revised English Bible © 1989 by permission of Oxford and Cambridge University Presses: pages 19, 21, 28, 34, 37, 46.

Picture Acknowledgments

1: The Bodleian Library, Oxford, MS E.D. Clarke 10, Byzantine illumination, Gospels c.1100.
2/3, 4, 6, 7, 11, 15, 18, 22, 35, 36, 44 and cover (St James): The Bodleian Library, Oxford, MS Auct. T. inf. 1.10, Byzantine illumination, 'Codex Ebnerianus', Constantinople, early 12th century.
9, 17, 25, 33, 41, 48: The Bodleian Library, Oxford, MS Canon Gr. 110, Byzantine illumination, Acts and Epistles, Constantinople, mid 10th century.

Series editor: Philip Law

Project editor: Angela Handley

Book designer: Nicholas Rous

Jacket designer: Gerald Rogers